S0-AKS-479

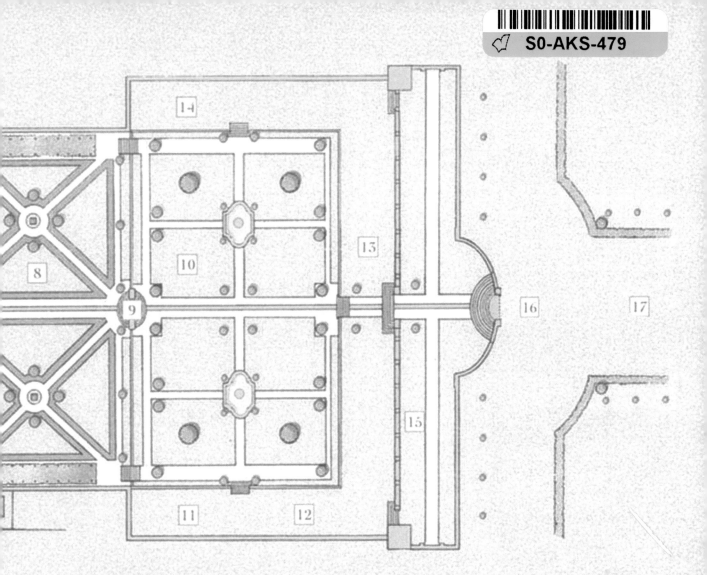

50 METRES

11	Rapsberries.
12	Box nursery.
13	Pavilion terrace.
14	Vegetable garden.
15	Fountain terrace.
16	Iron gate by Isaac Geslin — XVIIth C.
17	The hill vista — S.E.
18	Church XIVth C. Dedicated to St. Anne.
19	Rose garden.
20	Holy spring.
21	Greenhouse (Private).

The Gardens of Brécy

A Lasting Landscape

ÉRIC T. HASKELL

Photographs by
PASCAL HINOUS
and
ÉRIC T. HASKELL

Les Éditions du Huitième Jour

"The finery of an Italian princess thrown over the shoulders of a little Normandy peasant girl."

[Jacques de Lacretelle]

Table of Contents

Brécy: A Bird's Eye View

Ever since Adam and Eve were expelled from Paradise, mankind has been striving to recreate Eden on earth. Brécy is indeed such a recreation. An idealized vision of the world in which order and symmetry reign, this garden is an earthly haven far from the chaos of imperfection. Brécy possesses all of the attributes of the *hortus closus*. Within its privileged precincts reign an inspired tranquility and a sense of perfection that typify enclosed landscapes whose walls hold nature at bay in order to preserve rarified visions inside. The genius of this place offers even more, however. A terrestrial Eden, but one with celestial aspirations, Brécy seems to resist gravity.

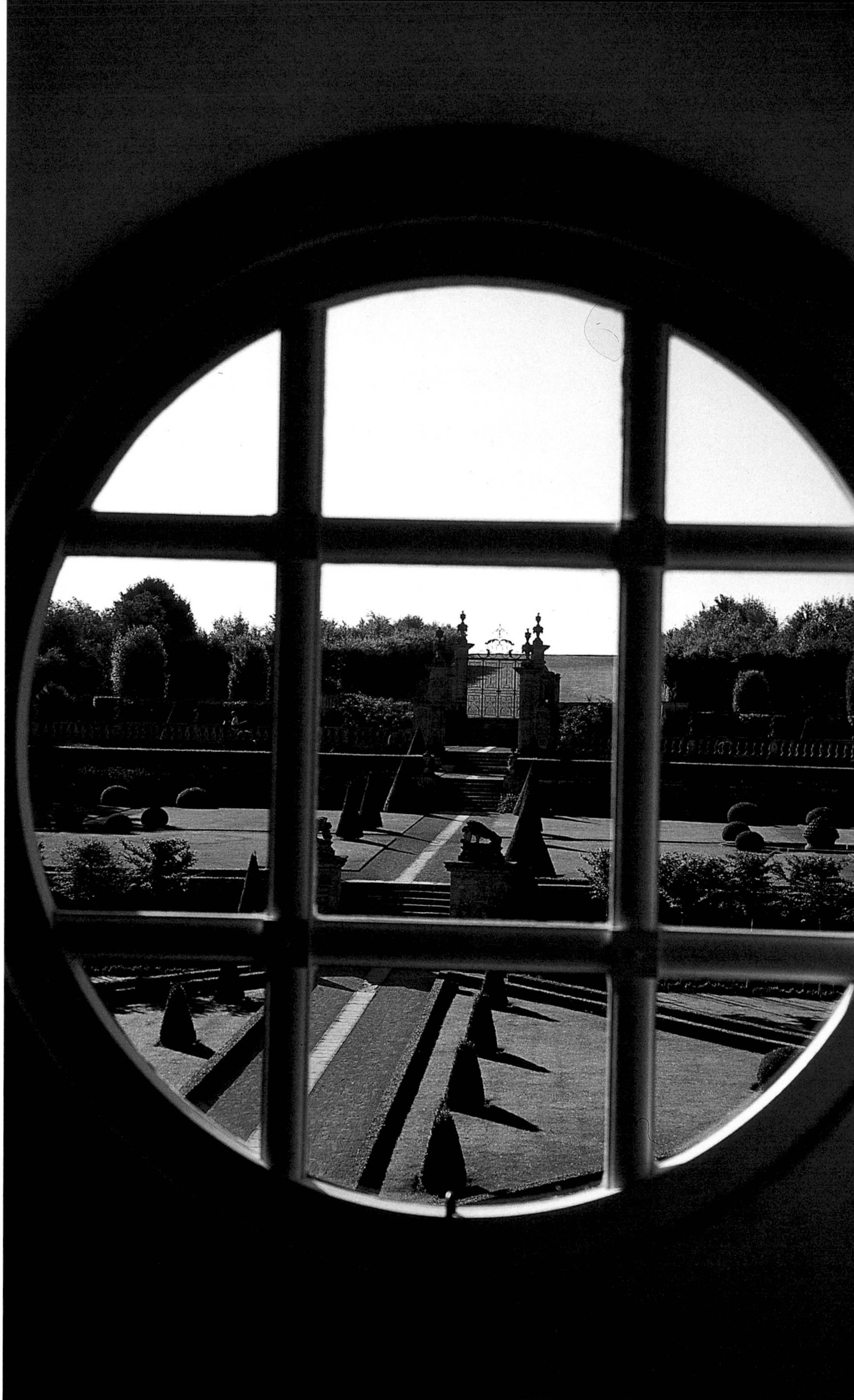

Above, left: Brécy's Gardens in 1946.

| A SEVENTEENTH-CENTURY GARDEN

As the garden's axial line stretches from the château's back façade to ascend a series of verdant terraces, it swiftly bursts through the monumental gate at the site's southeast boundary and soars into the infinitude of the sky. Terrestrial and celestial realms suddenly intersect in this inimitable paradigm of unity. The result is visual theatricality par excellence.

Poised at the threshold of a new landscape order, this garden's Medieval and Renaissance roots propose innovative notions of Baroque formality that are the hallmark of seventeenth-century garden design as well as France's most significant contribution to the aesthetics of landscape.

Although the gardens of Brécy were laid out during the seventeenth century, records are vague or inexistent, and much remains unknown about their precise beginnings. One thing that is certain, however, is that by the dawn of the twentieth century, the gardens were in a ruinous state, soon to be lost forever. At mid-century, an attempt was made to rectify this deplorable situation, but it would not be until the eve of the new millennium that Brécy would reawaken like a botanical Sleeping Beauty. An ongoing plan of restoration of both the château and the grounds has brought unparalleled beauty back to this site. Once on the verge of becoming a paradise lost, Brécy is now an exemplary vision of paradise regained.

Bird's Eye View
of Brécy in 2006.

I A PRIVILEGED LOCATION

Perfectly sited within a stretch of gently rolling terrain near Bayeux, in close proximity to the English Channel, Brécy is privileged by a temperate climate. Normandy has long been associated with superb gardens, and this precinct of Basse Normandie is particularly rich in examples.

None, however, possess a more eloquent articulation of formalist aesthetics than Brécy. The site's inherent surprise factor is particularly fetching. Because it is partially hidden in its own diminutive vale, the visitor happens upon Brécy unexpectedly. The visual seduction is at once immediate and irresistible. Although but a few hours drive from Paris today, in the seventeenth-century, Brecy's distance from the capital would have taken days to travel. Early visitors were no doubt bowled over by the sophistication of this gem of a garden situated on such a far-flung margin of Île de France culture. Even today, the striking refinement and Cartesian logic of this landscape remain anomalous in the pastoral symphony of the surrounding landscape, known as the *bocage normand*. Furthermore, the specific placement of the estate, at the bottom of the dell in which it is situated, allows the garden to flourish in the protected enclave of a microclimate whose benefits are multiple, all the more so thanks to its southeastern exposure. This is, of course, the same placement that makes possible the landscape's axial drama, as it transcends from terrestrial to celestial domains.

The Château de Brécy seen from the *tapis vert*.

Through the grand gateway, the four terraces descend toward the château.

History and Myth

Much of Brécy's early history is based on incomplete archives, spotty records or supposition. Richard I is purported to have been the first Seigneur of Brécy during the second half of the twelfth century. Traces of medieval foundations dating from that period remain on the site.

I EARLY HISTORY

Departmental archives suggest that the present château was most likely built sometime between 1626 and 1636 for one Philippe Labbey, whose name often appears in archival materials as Labbé, by an unknown architect. It was sold to Jacques I Le Bas in 1638. The construction is clearly Louis XIII in style, whereas the monumental entry portal to the forecourt and the formal gardens, whose timbre is Baroque in character, are thought to have been a later addition to the site by Le Bas who, we believe, commissioned them in the late 1660s. Although the manor may have been built by a master mason, the portal as well as the gardens appear to be the work of a sophisticated architect. In terms of the landscape, this individual seems to have been familiar with contemporary aesthetic contours in vogue at court. Thanks to Le Nôtre's completion of Vaux-le-Vicomte in 1661 and the commencement of his work at Versailles the following year, the 1660s were a particularly prolific decade in the history of the French garden. With the assumption that Le Bas would have had Brécy's gardens laid out late in the decade, his choice of architect indicates that his tastes were more in harmony with cutting-edge courtly aesthetics than with the era's charming, but less grand, provincial modes of landscape design.

Jacques I Le Bas must have been quite a formidable character. His many titles – Seigneur of Cambes, Dean of the Aides to the Présidial of Caen, Chevalier of the Military Order of Saint-Louis and Commander of the Capitainerie – suggest a successful career. Until the year before his death, in 1674, he continued acquiring surrounding parcels of land in order to enlarge his estate, which he left to his son, Jacques II Le Bas.

Remarkably, Brécy remained in the Le Bas Family for almost two centuries. It was often passed through the family's eldest daughter, until it finally came into the possession of Marie-Henriette d'Angerville d'Aucher, who died without issue in 1827.

Opposite page:
A finial supported by four eagles enhances Brécy's rich ornamental agenda.

Above:
In the formal precincts, the passage from one terrace to the next is finely articulated in stone.

I THE ACTRESS, THE *ACADÉMICIEN*, AND THE GARDEN LOVER

A curious trend appears with the successive owners of Brécy.[1] Most neglected the estate in favor of other residences of note that they possessed. With the demise of the Le Bas dynasty, Brécy was acquired by the Lecreps family who allowed it to fall into a lamentable state. The gardens were all but abandoned, and the manor's condition was nothing short of perilous. In 1912, while driving through the Normandy countryside, Rachel Boyer passed in front of Brécy's monumental entrance, peered inside, fell in love with the place, and immediately purchased it. Because of Boyer's star status – she was a celebrated actress, *sociétaire* of the Comédie Française, and president of the Union des Arts – her acquisition of Brécy became headline news. This was the first time in the history of the estate that it drew public attention. Boyer's association with Brécy was a fortuitous one, and she worked closely with Victor Ruprich-Robert of the Monuments Historiques to insure the site's longevity. The focus of their interest, however, was in restoring the house. The gardens would have to wait their turn until three owners later!

Under subsequent proprietors – Boyer's nephew, Marcel Lefèvre, then Paul Maillot – Brécy once again suffered serious neglect until, in 1955, the property fell into the caring hands of Jacques de Lacretelle, who worked at renovating both the house and the garden. Novelist and member of the Académie Française, Lacretelle lectured and wrote about Brécy.[2] He tirelessly cleared the jumble of weeds and brambles under which the garden lay, then traced the diagonals of the first terrace, and dug the basins of the second. Lacretelle was assisted by Paul Leroy, architect for the Monuments Histo-riques, who made such appropriate additions as the handsome sundial on the interior wall of the monumental entrance portal. The Lacretelle family possessed other properties in the area, including the neighboring Château de Lantheuil. Once they purchased the Château d'O in the southern part of Basse Normandie, however, their interests shifted away from Brécy, which was then estate was rented out.

The most recent chapter in the history of Brécy – and the one that signals its modern renaissance – began in 1992, when it was acquired by Didier and Barbara Wirth. Although Boyer and Lacretelle were instrumental in saving the site, the Wirth's passion for the place has brought it into the twenty-first century with verve and a certain *art de vivre* that has been unequalled, perhaps even since Brecy's infancy. Their gargantuan efforts have transcended mere refurbishing to include the most meticulous aspects of historic restoration. In the vast program of works they have launched, both house and garden have undergone significant renovation.

Opposite page:
Portal frames the bell tower of Sainte-Anne-de-Brécy as a a Francis E. Lester rose blooms in the foreground.

[1] The chronology of Brécy's proprietors has been carefully established by Elizabetta Cereghini in
Brécy : Gentilhommière et jardins.
[2] See Lacretelle entries in bibliography.

One of a pair
of monumental
portals leading from
the parterre garden;
this one goes toward
Sainte-Anne-de-Brécy.

An early photo
of the monumental
portal leading out
of the parterre garden
toward the old bread oven.

Along with extensive work on the interior of the château and the addition of a remarkable library, the roof has been replaced. In the midst of this massive project, traces of an original octagonal-shaped cupola that once coiffed the manor were found in the beams. Now rebuilt, this belvedere offers breathtaking views of the gardens and surrounding countryside. It also restores elegance to the manor.

Of all of the works accomplished since 1992, however, those completed in the garden constitute the most significant contribution to the recasting of Brécy's original physiognomy. As a massive drainage system was installed, telephone and electrical lines were buried underground so that no modern elements would be visible to interfere with the garden's period feel. Eleven stone staircases, integral to the architectural success of the formal landscape, were painstakingly repaired. New additions, such as the first terrace's hornbeam *berceau* ("cradle"), the second terrace's paired fountains and the *tapis vert* ("green carpet") that extends majestically beyond the southern gates, have brought fresh beauty to the site. Furthermore, they are in the spirit of the original aesthetic agenda's subtle fabric.

This page:
The cupola atop
the château is framed
here by the arch
of the monumental
entry portal.

Opposite page:
The grand stair leads
from the fourth garden
terrace, through
the great gate, and
to the *tapis vert* beyond.

| MYTH AND LEGEND

Trying to retrace the history of Brécy's gardens is a daunting task. Incomplete period descriptions, inadequate maps and incoherent site analysis amount to a myriad of missing pieces in an often complex puzzle. The dearth of historic documentation was further exacerbated by the loss of Departmental Archives in the World War II bombing of Caen. Incomplete records have led to considerable misunderstanding about the beginnings of Brécy and to the fabrication of myths about the place, some of which have taken legendary proportions. First and foremost of these is the attribution of the house and gardens to François Mansard. There was indeed a marriage between the Burgundian branch of the Le Bas Family and the daughter of Jules-Hardouin Mansard. François Mansard worked at the nearby Château de Balleroy, built for Jean de Choisy between 1623 and 1636 and contemporary with the first phase of construction at Brécy. But a connection between the celebrated architect and Le Bas's modest manor has never been substantiated.

Another false notion is that the château and grounds were conceived of and constructed in a single phase. An educated eye suffices to dispel this tale. More outlandish still is the Décaris document that mistook, on an early cadastral map, the ensemble of buildings that form the farm at Brécy for the château complex itself, perpetuating yet further misconceptions over time. As recently as 1999, Deterville states, without any documentation whatsoever, that the gardens were constructed in 1653 to celebrate the wedding of François Le Bas.

When Jacques de Lacretelle acquired Brécy, he lamented that no archives were passed on to him. His words perhaps best sum up the puzzling past of this seigniorial seat: *"Pour ma part, je me fais l'effet d'un M. Jourdain qui se pavane orgueilleusement dans une maison dont il ignore l'origine et les secrets passés"*[3] ("As for me, I feel like a Monsieur Jourdain strutting proudly around a house of whose origin and secret past he is ignorant."). This playful reference to Molière's *Bourgeois Gentilhomme* serves to underscore the dilemma posed by insufficient archival materials. Difficulty in retracing historical fact has, of course, made the process of restoration particularly problematic. Nevertheless, in the case of Brécy, conjecture and enigma, as exemplified by the Mansard connection, have seemingly added to the appeal of the place, as myth has so often succeeded in conjuring up legend.

Opposite page:
This anonymous
19th century drawing
of the monumental
entrance to the château's
forecourt shows
the old thatched roofs
of the outbuildings.
Drafted and engraved
by Alexandre Maugendre,
1862.

[3] Jacques de Lacretelle in "La destinée d'un château historique: Brécy en Calvados", *Vieilles maisons françaises n°42*, p.17.

The Forecourt and the Château

Niched between the plains of Caen and Bayeux, at the bottom of the Seulles River valley, far from major roads and partially hidden from all who pass, the manor and especially the gardens of Brécy startle the viewer who happens upon them for the first time. In such a remote setting, their splendor is disarming, their elegance an enchantment. The seductive nature of Rachel Boyer's *coup de coeur* for the site is ever present for the visitor who turns into the long avenue leading to the château. As the monumental entrance gate comes into view, one imagines the surprises in store ahead.

I THE EXUBERANT PORTAL

Framed by Ionic pilasters and surmounted by a curved fronton with a notable tympanum, the arc de triomphe, as former owner Jacques de Lacretelle called it, is utterly unexpected in this rural setting. Although the family coat of arms is missing from the portal's central cartouche – a loss no doubt incurred during the Revolution – the massive oak doors retain their original ornamentation, including sculpted heads, cornucopias and gadroons. The elaborately carved tympanium above, the refinement of the friezes and spandrels, the quality of the bas-relief sculpture with its reeds and arabesques, and the flanking pilasters along the wall crowned by their handsome stone floral vases constitute an architectural ensemble of note. Lacretelle was on the mark in calling it *"une veritable page de Pierre"*[4] ("a veritable page of Stone").

As such, it succeeds effectively in prefiguring the architectural quality of what we might call Brécy's chapter of stone. This, of course, is the formal garden ahead, as yet still completely hidden from view. The façade's front door, now seen across the forecourt, reiterates in subtle terms the entrance portal's floral exuberance with the decorative device of a hand reaching down from the sky holding a cornucopia of fruit and flowers. This in turn prefaces the exuberance of the gardens. Indeed, the floral cornucopias, symbols of paradise, ingeniously establish the theme of transcendence so central to the aesthetics of ascent within the formal gardens beyond.

The proportions of the manor's façade are pleasing in their symmetry but decidedly modest in relation to the entrance portal. With its two stories of five windows each and a third featuring five dormers and an eye-catching cupola, the house is far less regal than its entry gate. The outbuildings, which connect the entrance arch to the house, originally contained barns, stables and a cider press. Until the early twentieth century, they were covered with thatch and had the quaint allure of a *ferme ornée*. Their picturesque aspect must have presented quite a visual jolt as the visitor passed through the monumental arch into the forecourt. It seems that from Le Bas's arrival on, Brécy was to be a site of ever-enticing juxtapositions.

Above:
Sculptural details from Brécy's monumental portal. The center image shows the hand on the tympanum above the château's front door.

[4] Jacques de Lacretelle, "Cinq châteaux normands entre Bayeux et Caen", *Association Basse-Normandie*, numéro spécial, p. 51.

Brécy's entry portal
and monumental carved
wooden doors frame
the château's façade,
coiffed by its cupola.

CÔTÉ COUR / CÔTÉ JARDIN

Jean de La Varende has called Brécy *"…le plus énigmatique des ensembles archi-tecturaux du Calvados"*[5] ("… the most enigmatic of architectural ensembles in the Calvados region"). Incomplete archives are one reason. Another is doubt-lessly the disparate stylistic tone between the magnificence of the entrance arch and the simplicity of the manor. Whereas the former resounds like a veri-table Te Deum, the latter resonates like a countrified melody. The massive Baroque entry appears to be a stage set, placed as it is before the modest yet harmonious façade of the manor, which seems more at home here amongst the rolling hillsides, shady glades and old farmsteads. Brécy's magic, due in part to the dynamics of surprise, is inextricably linked to the bucolic demeanor of its rural environs. Above all, these dynamics depend on the pairing of unexpected refinement with the pastoral simplicity of the site.

It was perhaps in order to demonstrate his ascending social prominence that Le Bas sought to gentrify the modest *gentilhommière* he had purchased in 1638, whose construction was then but a decade old. The addition of the grand entrance portal and the extensive formal gardens successfully accom-plished this, at the same time articulating his personal ambitions eloquently. His additions, clearly the work of a talented designer, are aesthetically in tune with each other. Architectural similarities exist between the two: the curved tympanum of the court portal,[6] for example, is echoed in the formal garden's handsome matched doorways flanking the parterre level. Such details bring unity to the *côté cour – côté jardin* (entrance court – back garden) ensemble. Some speculate that Le Bas had fallen on hard times, and that he settled for gussying up the entrance and adding the impressive landscape in order to mask the relative simplicity of the house. In either scenario, it seems safe to say that the gardens, rather than the manor, were the focus of the proprietor's passion. Brécy triumphs due to the sheer elegance of its landscape's origina-lity. One might, in fact, advance the idea that the house functions as a needed pause between the grandeur of the monumental entrance arch and the visual fireworks waiting just beyond. With this concept in mind, Le Bas was perhaps even subtler in conceiving his overall plan for the estate than we have credited him for to date.

Opposite page: View of the second and third terraces toward the box nursery and the raspberry plot.

[5] La Varende, *Châteaux de Normandie, Itinéraire Sentimental*, Plon, 1958, p. 172.
[6] There is a notable stylistic link between the entrance portal and wall consoles at Brécy and the chapel ornamentation at l'Isle Marie, located a few miles northwest of Carentan.

The Formal Gardens

The experience of stepping over the threshold into the formal gardens at Brécy is analogous to Alice's arrival in Wonderland. A more memorable sight is hard to imagine. Whereas the manor has the feel of countrified Louis XIII style, the grounds are transitional, yet ultimately under the spell of Sun King aesthetics.

| THE ITALIANATE FLAIR

Is this formality what prompted an anonymous reporter from the June 3, 1903 edition of *L'Eclair* to call Brécy "…*un petit Versailles perdu à travers les champs*" ("a little Versailles lost among the fields")? *Little* is the operative term here, for the entire house and garden occupy a single hectare. Brécy captures the infinite in the finite.

Enclosed on the northwestern perimeter by the house and on the others by walls whose only permanent opening is through the great gate at the southeastern edge, the garden appears at first glance to be entirely secluded. This feeling is dispelled as soon as the eye becomes fully engaged in the sumptuous visual scenario. Like giant steps, Brécy's four terraces ascend to the southeast. They are intersected by a strong axial path, whose function is to lead the eye toward the gate, up to the horizon and to the sky beyond. This axis is the backbone of the landscape as well as the design element that facilitates its single-point perspective. It is also the feature that amplifies the formal nature of the ensemble.

Yet while Brécy recalls in diminutive terms the formality of Vaux-le-Vicomte or Versailles, its specific brand of Sun King aesthetics seems nevertheless rooted in the fantasy of an Italian operetta. Sophisticated, yet full of charm. Noble, but with that *je ne sais quoi* of a comfortable allure. The Italianate flair of Brécy's formal landscape is due in part to the slope of its site, which recalls in a minor mode the great gardens of Italy, from the Villa d'Este to the Villa Lante.[7] One of seventeenth-century France's key contributions to the history of landscape design was the siting of noble estates on flat terrains. By not adopting this component of *grand siècle* gardening, Brécy retains a vaguely Italian flavor, irresistible in its appeal.[8]

[7] Many French Renaissance gardens, as exemplified by Gaillon, were also constructed on sloped sites. Most, however, situated the manor in such a way that it dominated the garden from above. The particular charm of Brécy resides in the placement of the manor at the bottom of the terrain. This constitutes an intriguing reversal of the usage widely in vogue during the sixteenth century in France.
[8] Marie-Françoise Valéry refers to Brécy as "…cet élégant poème italien dont les vers sont rythmés comme des alexandrins" ("*that elegant Italian poem whose verses have the rhythm of alexandrines*") in "Normandie : le jardin de Brécy", *Maison et Jardin*, novembre 1995.

I Brécy's Theatricality

Brécy has the fascination of an opulent theatrical set. At any moment, a dramatic performance seems ready to unfold. If the introductory parterre and four connected terraces are like the acts of the drama, then the eleven staircases connecting them are akin to the intricacies of plot articulation, and the ensemble promises a formidable dénouement in its grand southeastern exit gate. The magnificence of the multiple terraces is enhanced by a vast sculptural program that makes Brécy one of the most luxuriously furnished gardens of Europe. Seemingly endless sets of retaining walls and stone balustrades announce the succession of terraces. Upon them, legions of ornate *pots à feu* ("firepots") vie with finely carved vases of flowers and fruit in an array of decorative elements, ever-theatrical in their visual allure. This theatricality is at once central to Brécy's formal aesthetic and its most distinguishing feature. Perhaps its most memorable, too. On a par with the formal lexicon of other grand siècle gardens, Brécy's theatricality is further magnified by its confinement within walls and by its relatively small size.

Although we presume that these formal gardens were constructed in the late 1660s for Jacques I Le Bas, curiously, there is no existent documentation of the site until a century later. The 1772 parish map of the area, vaguely showing the gardens and their organization, is the first actual record we have of Brécy's landscape. It is not until the Napoleonic cadastre of 1811 that the plan of the garden appears sited within the walls of the estate. But even this archival reference is imprecise. Over time, specification of the terraces varies from three to four. What is certain, however, when we contemplate the configuration of the landscape today, is that whoever constructed Brécy's gardens had a keen understanding of the golden section, which is demonstrated here by the sophistication and elegance of the landscape's proportions. Cartesian rigor prevails throughout the articulation of the various precincts. This, along with refined optical illusions, makes for an overall result that is infinitely harmonious.

Despite the fact that the author of this site remains anonymous, Brécy's aesthetics are the work of someone who was well-educated, well-traveled and, above all, extremely knowledgeable about contemporary theories of landscape design. The vitality of Brécy's garden scheme speaks eloquently to this. And even if the landscape architect was less than well-versed in courtly taste, Le Bas, due to his governmental charge, must certainly have been acquainted with it. Furthermore, despite the unproven Mansard connection, Le Bas would have at least been familiar with Balleroy's handsome brand of formalism because of his family's link to its owner, Jean de Choisy.[9]

Opposite page:
Verdant and stone
architecture intersect
in this view of the second,
third and fourth terraces.

[9] This hypothesis by Braham and Smith appears in their study on *François Mansart*.

Brécy's terraces under snow as seen from the château's second floor.

Brécy's *tapis vert* is clearly visible beyond the great ironwork gate.

I THE TERRACES

Particularly intriguing are the subtle rhythms established by Brécy's terraces. From the intricate parterres of the first level, the landscape ascends to the sparse geometries of the last in a rich sequence of design experiences. Each possesses a definitive character, and each is a masterpiece in its own right. Moreover, the formalist agenda resonates with *élan* between the sculptural paradigm of hard and soft scape as exemplified by the stone ornaments and the verdant topiaries that occupy each level of the layout.

The first segment of the formal garden, situated immediately adjacent to and level with the southeast façade of the manor, serves as a brilliant preface to the four terraces beyond. This area's width mirrors the château's; the terraces, as we shall see, extend wider in their varied contours of enclosure. What makes this initial sector of the garden utterly unique is its striking *parterre de broderie*. Inspired by patterns from André Mollet's seventeenth-century *Le Jardin de Plaisir*,[10] the design is entirely appropriate for Brécy. First and foremost, the parterre inscribes this landscape within the aesthetic tradition of the *jardin à la française*. Neither pretentious nor overly ornate in relation to the modest lines of the manor's architecture, the parterre also serves as a visual extension of the ground-floor rooms – a sort of verdant carpet flung out from the *rez-de-chaussée* ("ground floor") in order to unify house and garden in a single, dazzling glance.

From this point, the eye ascends to the first terrace. Its retaining wall is appointed with an array of decorative sculptures, some topped with fruit and floral motifs, others with flames of stone. Their elegance is arresting. On this level, diagonal paths crisscross a pair of matching panels of lawn with obelisk topiaries marking their intersection. A stilt hedge shading the perimeter paths of this space is responsible for its appeal. A recent addition, this living pergola recalls the *berceaux* that abound in French formal gardens during the seventeenth and early eighteenth centuries. Placed as it is here, this verdant relief from the intensity of the sculptural agenda adds volume to the ensemble. The pleached *allée* also introduces the intimacy of overhead enclosure to the grand axial landscape, while softening its dominant linearity. Enhanced by a pair of whimsical chinoiserie benches along the northwest return walls, and other banquettes set under its hornbeam bowers, the *berceau* encourages one to linger under its shady canopy. It is a particularly eloquent player in the spatial interactions of the terrace ensemble.

[10] Brécy's parterre appears to have been inspired by the engraving that appears on page 23 of Mollet's *Le Jardin de Plaisir*.

The axial path of ascent again intersects paired panels of lawn as we arrive at the second terrace. Here again, paths cut across each panel, squaring them this time. Both have matched fountains at their centers. A pair of basins was initially set in place in 1960 by Lacretelle, but it was not until the recent addition of the fountains within them that the sound of water was introduced into the landscape. Symbolic of regeneration, water plays a crucial role in garden history, particularly in the tradition of the French formal landscape, where it was used to astonish the viewer while enhancing the iconographic agenda of royal retreats. At Brécy, the presence of water is a fortunate addition, entirely appropriate with the site's aesthetic ambiance. Composed of mounded artichokes, symbols of good fortune, these fountains, with their

cascading rivulets, bring the play of water to the tonal scenario, enriching its theatricality with the addition of both movement and musicality.

By optically effacing the difference in height between the two levels, aerial views of the garden make the first and second terraces appear as a single flat parterre composed of four grand lawn panels, each intersected by paths that eventually produce sixteen sections, eight triangular and eight square. This *trompe l'oeil* is particularly effective in associating Brécy with the sort of formalism synonymous with the greatest of France's seventeenth-century gardens. Viewed from the manor, however, the differentiation between the two levels is considerable. This accounts for Brécy's uncommon charm, as well as for its affinity with certain Renaissance ideals.

Brécy's parterre design, seen here in summer and in winter, was inspired by a pattern from Mollet's *Le Jardin de Plaisir*.

Opposite page: An aerial-hedged *allée* leads to the stair of the second terrace.

Above: One of a pair of artichoke fountains that animate the third terrace.

Opposite page: The parterre is viewed here from outside the walls of the garden's formal precinct.

Above: View from the third terrace toward the grand gateway to the *tapis vert*.

| Lions in the Landscape

A pair of finely carved stone lions, frozen in heraldic stance, serves to accentuate the change in grade between the first and second terraces. They also pose as icons of demarcation between the two. Symmetrically positioned on high pedestals halfway up the central staircase, these lions have the odd characteristic of possessing double heads. While one pair of heads faces the manor, the other focuses its gaze on the southeast gate. The effect is salient because they accentuate the landscape's axial thrust by virtue of their double gazes along the meridional line.

They are particularly effective in yet two other arenas. First, they repeat the pair of lions that flanks the grand portal at the estate's entrance, thus reiterating the aesthetic links between the *côté cour* and the *côté jardin*. Secondly, if the front pair serves as a rite of passage into the domain, the back pair seems to signal the exit as they look toward the great gate. Although their precise iconographical meaning is shrouded in mystery, the bicephalous lions might symbolize the rupture between terrestrial and celestial realms, between the garden of earthly delights and the infinity of the sky beyond.

Brécy's unique double-headed lions are situated between the first and second terraces.

| HIDDEN *POTAGERS*

The third terrace introduces an astute arrangement of special harmonies to the grand scheme of the garden. By enclosing the second level on three sides and concealing the returns behind high walls, matching parallel rectangles are created to accommodate a pair of *potagers*. Both are sited against the perimeter, and both are appointed with matching sets of stairs that descend to the terrace below. In line with the artichoke fountains, the path created makes for a sweeping cross-axial perspective that inventively reiterates the increases in grade of the central axis. These pocket kitchen gardens are cleverly concealed from the sight lines that extend from the manor up the central axis. This conceit allows for the complete retention of the formal ambiance, while wittily bringing an amiable appeal to the edges of the garden, reminding the visitor that the Norman countryside lies just beyond the surrounding walls. An eye for detail is ever present in the various precincts of the gardens, and these *potagers* are no exception. The artichokes cultivated here, for example, find their sculptural equivalent in the fountains of the terrace below and in the ornamentation of the nearby church's steeple. Brécy is replete with similarly shared associations that never fail to increase the refinement of our viewing experience.

If the delineation between the first and second terraces was marked by the drama of the bicephalous lions, the passage from the third to the fourth is just as notable, thanks to the stone balustrades that mark its entire cross-axial width. Composed of squared columns ornately inscribed with acanthus leaves, they are nothing short of princely in proportion. Their presence in the landscape, along with the twin pavilions situated in the southern corners of this terrace, account for the theatricality that perhaps inspired Lacretelle to refer to Brécy as a *"théâtre de Pierre"*.[11] At regular intervals atop the balustrade are placed sculpted ornaments that complement those of the entrance, flanking the portal, as well as those of the first terrace's retaining wall. Remarkable for the finesse of their execution and for their exceptional patina, these ornate sculptures serve the same function as the lions in unifying front and back landscapes. Their sheer number, along with the magnitude of the balustrade supporting them, draws the eye to this terrace and ingeniously prepares us for the *coup de théâtre* of the fourth and final terrace, just above.

The third and fourth terraces are considerably shallower than the first and second, so much so that the steps leading up to them seemingly collapse into a single stair, bypass their landing, and appear to be continuous. This accentuates the tension of the landscape's dramatic *dénouement* at the horizon ahead. These two terraces are also slightly pitched a few degrees forward in order to accentuate the theatricality of the optical illusion. Rhythms undergo slight changes in cadence, but the variations on the theatrical theme remain intact across the formal precincts of Brécy.

Opposite page:
From the potager at the edge of the second terrace, we look back to the château and the bell tower of Sainte-Anne-de-Brécy.

[11] Jacques de Lacretelle, "Cinq châteaux normands entre Bayeux et Caen,", p. 52.

I THE GRAND GATE

The fourth and final terrace is the last act of Brécy's landscape drama. As such, it performs in a majestic mode, bringing closure to a rich formalist scenario. The cross-axial paths of this terrace lead the eye northeast and southwest past notable collections of topiary to matching stone benches. Each is set against its wall within thuja arches that mimic the semi-circular vaults above them. The clever addition of the *trompe l'oeil* trellis-work *en perspective*, installed just above the benches, fills the topiary arches and allows the imagination to wander beyond the parameters of the garden.

Yet this cross-axial activity is but a minor intrigue in comparison to the major drama of the great wrought-iron gate that defines the southernmost edge of the garden. On it depends the final triumph of Brécy's theatricality. A stately set of piers, prefigured by those of the third terrace, are placed atop the last set of stairs within a grand exedra formed by the southern wall. The gate they support is heroic in scale, yet light and airy in conception. Upon close inspection, it seems far too grandiose for the garden. Viewed from the château, however, or from other terraces within the formal precincts, its proportions are appropriate and fitting for such a princely landscape. Lacretelle suggests that the gate may have been produced by a talented student of Isaac Geslin.[12] Whoever its author may have been, this is clearly the work of a master craftsman. The finely chased gateway, set as it is against the ascending horizon, seems to inscribe its decorative agenda in silhouette upon the sky. The interlaced initials "LR" placed within the cartouche coif refer to Jacques I Le Bas and his wife, Catherine Roger, under whose tenure the formal gardens at Brécy were built. And although the family coat of arms[13] does not appear here, the elements that compose it, such as balustrades, acanthus leaves and the sky-blue color, are apparent throughout the architectural agenda of the landscape. Erased from the tympanum of the entrance arch during the Revolution, the family crest could not be effaced from the garden's symbolic underpinnings, where it still resides potently. Clearly, the wrought-iron initialing reminds us that we are in the domain of the Le Bas Family, and under the spell of its creator's *chef d'œuvre*.

Opposite page:
Conical topiary prefigure
the monumental
gates of the third
and fourth terraces.

---

[12] Jacques de Lacretelle, "Cinq châteaux normands entre Bayeux et Caen,"., p. 58.
[13] "On an azure-colored background, a golden strip is accompanied by three shells surmounted by silhouetted balustrades and surrounded by acanthus leaves", E. Cereghini, *Brécy, gentilhommière et jardins*.

Flanking the initialed cartouche and draped over it are lavish quantities of acanthus leaves alluding to those of the balustrade bases and decorative scroll supports prominently displayed in *bas-relief* throughout the garden. But the crowning device of the cartouche is perhaps the most eye-catching of all. A floral profusion of delicate *clochettes* rises from the initials in a flourish that recalls a bouquet of fireworks. This decorative gesture replicates a device found atop many of the garden's stone vases. More importantly, it is aesthetically linked to the *pots à feu* that are placed right and left upon the high piers. According to Lacretelle, an admiring visitor once said of these firepots that their flames were *"une sorte de panache final dans un feu d'artifice de pierres"* ("a sort of final panache in the fireworks of stone").[14]

What is most beguiling about this comment is the notion that Brécy's sculptural agenda recalls – albeit in a less-grandiloquent mode – the fireworks so frequently presented in the great aristocratic gardens of the period where fêtes proliferated on an epic scale. Here, these *pots à feu*, the most monumental of the garden, join others atop the entrance walls, the retaining walls of the first terrace and the grand balustrades of the third, to remind us that this is a décor for spectacle and for all that is spectacular.

Opposite page:
The grand gate's shadow falls upon the *tapis vert* on a late summer afternoon.

[14] Jacques de Lacretelle, "Cinq châteaux normands entre Bayeux et Caen,", p. 58.

| THEMATICS OF ASCENT

Brécy's grand gates do not close the formal gardens. Instead, they open them to the horizon, extend the axial line, and lengthen the perspective to include the *tapis vert* beyond until it eventually intersects with the sky above. They constitute the liberating force of the ensemble. Without them, Brécy would still reflect Medieval and Renaissance modes but could not express the aspirations of the Baroque mindset that seeks transcendence to realms beyond reality. In order to facilitate this notion of transcendence, the axial path extends beyond the gate and up the adjacent hillside. Supporting this design, a double hornbeam *allée* lines the verdant avenue as it climbs to the horizon. Quoted directly from Le Nôtrean vocabulary, as exemplified by Vaux-le-Vicomte's *allée* and *tapis vert* that lead the eye above the grand cascades and off into the distance, Brécy's axial prolongation is more abrupt in its ascent, more startling in its effect. Furthermore, because the eye is not distracted by any statuary, such as Vaux's Hercules, the visual immediacy of Brécy's horizon line makes for an almost heady encounter with the sky beyond.

During its restoration, nine feet of earth were added to the slope. This astute addition, along with the combination of increased slope and framing *allée*, exaggerates the foreshortening, increasing the illusion and heightening the visual impact. Two transitions are thus seamlessly accomplished: first the one between the geometric garden and the surrounding landscape, then the one between the terrestrial and celestial realms. The amplified foreshortening adds yet another page to the chapter of optical illusions that, in the spirit of Le Nôtre's *trompe l'oeil* techniques, reinforce Brécy's original theatricality. If the southeastern gate provides the liberating force for the beholder of the grand axis, it also serves the imperative role of visually giving the garden back to Nature. We have come full circle in the symbolic network of this landscape. Thus the divine hand sculpted over the front door, which reaches down from the heavens with its floral tribute, eventually reclaims its bequest.

| AN ABOUT-FACE

Lest we overlook one of Brécy's most enchanting vistas, we must do an about-face and view the gardens and manor from the grand gateway. Looking north-west, the terraces again appear to be a vast stair that now descends toward the château – from the grandeur of the highest, at the gate, to the intimacy of the lowest, at the parterre – in a rich sequence of experiences. From this vantage point, the harmony engendered by the axial configuration takes on new meaning. What suddenly becomes clear is that the house is actually situated between two grand portals, one at the entrance, one at the exit, and that the unifying agent is the axial path that begins well in advance of the former and ends well beyond the latter.

The magical component here, of course, is that due to refined geometry and clever illusion, it never really ends. The intersection with the horizon prevents closure. This is, of course, why Brécy's dramatic scenario is ultimately infinite.

Opposite page: View of the terraces, the château, and Sainte-Anne-de-Brécy from the great gate at the top of the formal garden.

04 | THE FORMAL GARDENS

I A DISPLACED CENTER AND *GRAND SIÈCLE* GEOMETRIES

Herein lies the principal reason for which this landscape remains aesthetically akin to the Baroque. Medieval and Renaissance gardens turned their focus inward to their center. For the most part, the central motif had to do with water, whether in the simplicity of countless Medieval cloister pools or in a Renaissance extravagance such as Gaillon's celebrated St. John the Baptist fountain. The focus was on the interior rather than the exterior, on inward rather than outward spatial dimensions. In sync with the Baroque aesthetic and its notions of transcendence and mobility of spirit, the seventeenth century radically displaces the center of the garden and relocates it outside the traditional parameters.

This is indeed the case at Brécy. As the intentionality of the design reigns supreme, the eye – unable to find the center of the formal scape – is seduced into taking part in the ascent, eventually folding its gaze into the heavens. If upon a cursory glance, the eye mistakes the pair of two-headed lions for the center of the garden, the error is immediately corrected. Their gaze is so carefully calibrated to emphasize the controlling axis that they resolutely resist playing the role of *point de mire* by ushering the eye rapidly past them and up toward the exit portal.

The single-point perspective at work in the optical scheme of Brécy further facilitates axial seduction. Inextricably linked to the lexicon of the formal garden, it forces the eye to constantly refocus on the wrought-iron gate from all vantage points throughout the garden. This ingenious device again amplifies the dramatic score, transporting the viewer to another world beyond the gateway and up the *allée*. At Vaux-le-Vicomte, the single-point perspective is intended to draw our attention to the mighty statue of the Farnese Hercules, associating the demi-god's grandeur with that of Nicolas Fouquet, Minister of Finance during the early reign of Louis XIV.

At Versailles, the perspectival agenda is once again of a political nature. As courtiers move about the grounds, the royal presence is revealed to them as the setting sun produces a blinding illumination upon the *grand canal*. Sun King symbolism is here at its zenith. The intention of Brécy's brand of single-point perspective, however, is more poetic than political. It is also egoless. Its aspirations are comparatively quite simple. They seem to remind us that earthly existence is fleeting, that even the geometrical perfection of such an ensemble as Brécy possesses the underlying fragility of the finite, and that transcendence is central to their concerns. Perhaps Barbara Wirth's expression of this essence is the most concise of all: *"Les soirs d'été le soleil se couche dans l'axe du portail et allume le jardin. Instant parfait."*[15] ("On summer evenings, the sun sets in the axis of the portal and illuminates the garden. A perfect instant."). In this fleeting *coup de théâtre*, Brécy's spectacle is suddenly complete.

Opposite page:
The path leads
from Sainte-Anne-de-Brécy
to the exterior walls
of the formal garden
and the terraces beyond.

[15] Every year on the twenty-first of June, the sun rises on a perfect axial line with Brécy's monumental entrance arch and sets precisely centered on the great gate. At that very instant, the significance of the controlling axial line is accentuated and the magnificence of the ensemble is underscored with *élan*.

Brécy's Plant Palette

Even though Brécy's parish map of 1772 vaguely alludes to the garden and its layout, no archival information related to the original plantings has been located to date. One easily imagines that the site would have been the subject of any number of articles in the local horticultural society bulletins that proliferated during the nineteenth century. But by then, the formal aesthetic was so hopelessly out of vogue that Brécy seems to have been simply passed over in favor of the new naturalistic landscapes.

| MINERAL AND VEGETAL ARCHITECTURE

In 1845, M. du Méril, President of the Horticultural Society of Caen, affirmed that "the discredit of old ideas (formal garden design) is complete".[16] What appears evident is that the cutting-edge technology currently being pioneered in the field of garden archeology offers the sole key to a complete understanding of Brécy. Only this resource could inform us of the precise nature and configuration of the garden's original plantings.

We can surmise that, given the extent of Brécy's mineral and architectural components, the vegetal accompaniment must have been similarly elaborate. As the current owner has justly stated "to this profusion of mineral architecture must respond a profusion of vegetal architecture".[17] An intelligent balance between the two is imperative. And the selection of plant materials, without period records, has to be done with *savoir-faire*. This is an interpretive task. Lacretelle understood this principle when he planted the *parterre de broderie*. Fortunately, at Brécy, the plethora of garden architecture that has so miraculously survived to date offers a host of clues as to which plant materials are aesthetically fitting for the period and style of the landscape.

Opposite page:
The borders of
the second terrace
in early spring.

Above:
Poppies *Romneya Coulteri*
of the second terrace's
border in full summer
bloom.

[16] « ...le discrédit des anciennes idées (jardin régulier) est complet. »
   M. du Méril, quoted in Cereghini, *Brécy : Gentilhommière et Jardins*.
[17] « À cette profusion d'architecture minérale doit répondre une profusion d'architecture végétale »
   As quoted in Valéry, Marie-Françoise, "Normandie : Le Jardin de Brécy," *Maison et Jardin*, November 1995.

I RENOVATIONS AND NEW ADDITIONS

As for the colossal projects – the reforestation along the approach to the château, the formal configuration of lindens before the entrance portal, the extension of the axial line past the grand gate with its *tapis vert* and double hornbeam *allée* – all are in sync with the ensemble, with Le Nôtrean aesthetics, and with *grand-siècle* landscaping. If they were not original to the site, they should have been.

The less Herculean projects are just as ambitious in their objective of reviving details of the period ambiance within the garden. The Versailles boxes, for example, with their holly and boxwood clipped in lollipop shapes, furnish the parterre area and ease the transition from interior to exterior.

The abundance of topiary throughout the terraces creates a rich dialogue between the geometries of the hardscape and verdant sculpture of the softscape, and the former is relaxed by the latter. This serves to dissipate the sometimes solemn physiognomy of Baroque gardens, whose plants are often eclipsed by architecture. At Brécy, an elegant array of obelisks, pyramids, pilasters, spirals, columns, cones and balls in every imaginable dimension activate the eye, inviting it to dart about the garden with rapture. Period engravings of the bosquets of Versailles and other great gardens of the era show a profusion of similar topiary shapes, legions of which are presented in boxes as smart as Brécy's. Composed of yew, box and bay, these topiaries match the spirit of the sculptural agenda and invigorate it. Additional evergreen plantings, such as Mexican orange, sweet olive, Italian buckhorn and Portuguese laurel make certain that, even in the dead of winter, the garden retains a hint of its leafy mantle.

The modern addition of Jekyllian[18] borders to the second terrace has further relaxed the hardscape. The color palette used here, restricted to greens, whites and blues, is very discreet. In a parallel fashion, abundant clematis and a legion of climbing roses dress often stark walls and perform as elegant players in the horticultural scene . Finally, the three miles of hedges recently installed outside the walls of the estate re-establish its once verdant frame, which was sadly lost to the Dutch elm disease that ravaged the site during the second half of the twentieth century. Once again, the domain has taken on a lushness entirely in keeping with its spirit. In doing so, Brécy has fortunately reclaimed what La Varende referred to as its *"inexplicable magnificence."*[19]

Opposite page:
Real and *faux* topiaries
watch over Barthélémy.

[18] Gertrude Jekyll (1843- 1932), landscape architect.
[19] As quoted in Lacretelle, "Cinq châteaux normands entre Bayeux et Caen", p.51.

Compartments for Conversation

Well off of the central axis and beyond the
formal precincts of Brécy discreetly resides its
most charming attribute. A constellation of
what might be called compartments for conver-
sation or even follies lies hidden behind the high
walls of the central garden. These sites, like so
many secluded retreats, are accessed solely
through gates set within the walls off the trans-
versal axes of the *parterre* level and the second
terrace.

| FOLLIES

There in its margins, they await discovery by the viewer in need of relief from the *grandeur* of the geometric landscape. Unlike the formal garden, they cannot be perceived in a single glance. Rather, their role in Brécy's scenario is to surprise. Additionally, they bring mystery and intimacy to the drama by heightening its theatricality in ways different from those we have seen in the initial steps of our promenade.

The eighteenth-century garden is replete with examples of follies. From pagodas to pyramids, from minarets to tartar tents, these structures transformed landscapes into dreamscapes. At the Folie Monceau or the Désert de Retz, the visitor is seduced by their exoticism and transported to otherworldly realms. Watteau's celebrated *Voyage à Cythère* epitomizes the escapist notion central to the aristocratic mindset that created these illusionary gardens.

Although Brécy contains in its margins minor references to these follies, as well as a direct quote in the striking shell décor of the third terrace's east pavilion,[20] they are far from the eclecticism of Chinese bridges and Roman colonnades. What we have here are disparate elements in the spirit of the eighteenth-century pleasure garden that lead the viewer off the formal paths for momentary divertissements. More in the mode of the *ferme ornée*, such as those at *Moulin Joli* or the *Hameau de la Reine* at Versailles, Brécy's follies are more picturesque than exotic. Some seem not even intentionally planned.

Such is the case of the old bread oven and its surrounding compartments situated just beyond the northeast wall of the parterre level of the formal gardens. A low rectangular building divided into two rooms *en enfilade* with the actual opening of the oven on axis with the entrance, the structure lost its roof long ago. In the whimsical spirit of the eighteenth century, it now appears as a quaint ruin. Tree peonies and hydrangeas furnish the interior, accessible via a central path. But what gives this postage stamp-sized Sissinghurst its singular allure is the mass of clematis that covers its walls and spills over into its center. Mixed with wisteria, this mantle shrouds the miniature building in mystery. Painterly in feel, enticing as a reverie, this is perhaps Brécy's most poetic interlude.

Situated beyond the southwest wall of the formal vista, a series of interlocking spaces holds similar surprises. A small path leads to the first encounter – an old greenhouse. Here, benches collapse under the weight of antique terra-cotta pots, each planted with unusual flora. Intimacy reigns along with a quiet charm, and the viewer feels less vulnerable than in the vast, open spaces of the formal garden. Just beyond the greenhouse, the path meanders into a hedged enclosure dedicated to children's activities. "Petit Brécy," a tiny blue playhouse with a slate roof, Dutch door, and window boxes surveys a sandbox while a brightly-painted dwarf looks on.

Preceding page:
The shell pavilion.

Opposite page:
Brécy's old bread oven was transformed into a garden folly early in the 20th century.

[20] In the spirit of Rambouillet's *pavillon de coquillages* and of other shell décors fabricated during the eighteenth-century, this work is in progress. Although situated in the formal precinct of the garden, the fantasy is held here in secret until the visitor actually penetrates the pavilion.

The touch of unexpected humor makes this a *sorbet* of garden sites. The juxtaposition of the intimate scale of these various compartments and the infinite perspectives located just over the wall adds to the overall suspense of the viewing experience at Brécy.

The most intricate and visually captivating of Brécy's small-scale spaces is the herb garden. Despite its location within the estate walls adjacent to the kitchen, this diminutive *jardin des simples* is nevertheless well off of the central axis. And although the formal landscape lies just beyond its stone balustrade, this garden is a charismatic parenthesis in the grand scheme of Brécy. Planted in a sophisticated checkerboard pattern interspersed with tubs of topiary laurel, the design is composed of thyme, tarragon, rosemary and mint. This parterre is centered on an antique wellhead that constitutes one of Brécy's premier garden ornaments. Four small columns, finely sculpted in the Tuscan manner, support the well's handsome domed cover. The quaint mood of the ensemble underscores the site's affiliation with the picturesque quality of its other follies, whose dual role is to serve both as *mises en appétit* for, and relief from the *pièce de résistance* of the grand formal landscape.

Opposite page:
The herb garden,
with its antique wellhead
sculpted in the Tuscan
manner, is adjacent
to the parterre garden.

This page:
Covered in clematis
Montana Wilsonii,
one of the pair
of pavilions on
the fourth terrace
doubles as a shell grotto
(see interior, p.72).

| SAINTE-ANNE-DE-BRÉCY

Finally, playing a related role, is Brécy's thirteenth-century part-Romanesque, part-Gothic church situated on the diagonal off the southwest side of the château. In the spirit of the borrowed view – so central to the vernacular of eighteenth-century landscape aesthetics – Sainte-Anne-de-Brécy functions admirably as an eye-catcher in the picturesque mode, especially when seen from the dais of the grand gateway and the upper terraces of the formal garden. This is the church that Rachel Boyer is purported to have purchased in 1914 for a mere 101 francs!

The pleasure gardens of the *Ancien Régime* built just prior to the Revolution had a fascination for Gothic architecture, because it responded to the Romantic obsession for religious ruins. The *cathédrale engloutie* at Bagatelle and the ruins of the chapel at the Désert de Retz exemplify this taste. Although the construction of Brécy's gardens precedes this stylistic vogue, the notion of the borrowed view is nevertheless present at the site. Perhaps in a more English than French manner, the vista toward the church comprises the ultimate in painterly landscapes.

Inside the church, inscribed on the gravestone of Jacques I Le Bas's daughter, Estelle, are the following words: *"Estelle, notre soeur bien-aimée, à toi qui a victorieusement surmonté l'épreuve de la mort, nous te dédions ce jardin, symbole de résurrection et de gloire"* ("Estelle, our beloved sister, to thee who victoriously overcame the trial of death, we dedicate this garden, symbol of resurrection and glory"). Elizabetta Cereghini believes that the gardens of Brécy may have been a tribute to Estelle, who died in 1671, from her two brothers, Jacques II Le Bas and Georges.[21] This hypothesis supports the notion that the formal landscape and its axial intersection with the sky may well indeed be inspired by the dialectics of ascent and perhaps even redemption. As such, Brécy might be considered a site of memory par excellence.

Opposite page:
The bell tower of
Sainte-Anne-de-Brécy
as viewed from
the second terrace.

[21] Cereghini, *Brécy: Gentilhommière et Jardins*, p. 156.

Brécy: a Lasting Landscape

Gardens are fragile markers of human aspirations. Architectural ensembles may last centuries with little care, but a landscape can disintegrate from only a few decades of neglect. Brécy's highs and lows have been nothing short of mercurial.

I « THIS LITTLE CORNER OF EARTH »

The initial architectural envelope of the site leads us to believe that the original seventeenth-century gardens must have been quite remarkable. Their extent and elegance surely astonished the visitor during their heyday, particularly due to the remoteness of their location in relation to Ile de France culture. Abandoned at the Revolution, the gardens continued on a steady downward spiral of decay during the nineteenth century. Written references to them in 1855, for example, note their derelict condition. During this period, agricultural production on the surrounding farms was accentuated over the upkeep of the landscape. This farming even encroached on the formal gardens, as can be seen in photographs from a 1907 edition of *La Vie à la Campagne* in which a kitchen garden thrives on the second terrace, while an orchard occupies the third. At the same time, the forecourt became a pigsty, given over entirely to barnyard animals.

Despite this disfiguration, the site somehow managed to retain a sufficient amount of its initial grandeur to continue to fire the imagination. An anonymous writer for the February 15, 1914 edition of *Le Miroir* refers to Brécy as *"… ce petit coin de terre où a fleuri, il y a déjà plus de deux siècles, le goût français le plus pur et où l'on retrouve la marque d'un génie harmonieux et souple, savant à plaire, ami de la mesure et de l'ordre"* ("… this little corner of earth where bloomed, already two centuries ago, the purest of French taste, in which one finds the mark of a harmonious and supple genius, intelligently pleasing, friend of measure and of order"). Given the dilapidated state of the château in the photographs accompanying the article, its author was certainly more in harmony with the genius of place than with its condition at the time.

Neglect of the site during the nineteenth century prompted an intervention by the Monuments Historiques in 1903 that listed the château's exteriors and garden. Rachel Boyer's work on the interiors facilitated their listing in 1914. Her efforts, as well as those of Jacques de Lacretelle, who worked at refurbishing both the manor and the landscape, saved the ensemble from complete dilapidation during the latter part of the twentieth century, until the Wirths took over. World War II and the Normandy invasion might well have sounded the death knell for Brécy. Situated just five miles south of Gold's Beach and directly on the corridor of the Allied advance of June, 1944, the domain was miraculously spared due to the fact that, by the evening of the first landings, the British Army had fortuitously passed beyond it. Despite the long and bitter battle to enter Caen, thirteen miles away, Brécy was not bombed, and no battles were waged in its immediate environs. However, like many of its neighbors, the château was successfully occupied by the Germans and the English.

The theatricality of the fourth terrace's balustrade enhances the view towards the château's south-east facade.

| BRÉCY TODAY

Today, Brécy has awoken from its slumber and regained its noble allure. Recent renovation, preservation and a host of appropriate additions give the site its present physiognomy. This is most perceptible in the astute balance that has been struck between Brécy's architectural and vegetal entities, now in perfect harmony. The verdant accompaniment of the landscape that reenergizes the once-stark linear monotony of the terraces was sorely lacking in volume due to decades of neglect. This equilibrium, so imperative to the aesthetic fabric of the place, has however been entirely revived. The formalist exercise resonates across each topiary, through every balustrade, and past the garden walls to the carefully calibrated orchards beyond. Furthermore, a veritable *art de vivre* characterizes every detail of the ensemble.

This is most striking when, in the early morning light, the gardens are viewed from the lofty cupola that crowns the central portion of the manor's roof. Allowing a three-hundred-sixty-degree view of the formal gardens, the follies and the surrounding countryside, the soaring panorama from the belvedere is a portrait of perfection. This view evokes what André Hallays referred to as Brécy's "charme singulier"[22] and what La Varende called its "inexplicable magnificence."[23]

In doing so, Brécy – one of the most handsome landscape ensembles of Europe and surely France's most notable small-scale formal garden – accomplishes its ultimate goal of ascent and thus moves triumphantly into the new millennium.

This earthly paradise, once on the verge of being lost, has now been miraculously regained.

Opposite page:
The front door of
the château with
its unique hand-motif
tympanium and
its friendly guardian.

[22] As quoted in Lacretelle, "La destinée d'un château historique: Brécy en Calvados", p. 17.
[23] As quoted in Lacretelle, "Cinq châteaux normands entre Bayeux et Caen", p. 51.

Selected bibliography

ANONYMOUS. "La Maison Seigneuriale de Brécy."
La Construction Moderne, October 17, 1885, and October 31, 1885.

ANONYMOUS. "Un petit Versailles perdu à travers les champs."
L'Eclair, June 3, 1903 and June 4, 1903.

ANONYME. "Au cours d'une promenade en auto, Mlle. Rachel Boyer découvre
et achète une église pour 101 Francs." *Le Miroir*, February 15, 1914.

ANONYME. "En Normandie, un jardin de lumière : Brécy."
Plaisir de France, October 1964, p. 51.

Marcus BINNEY. "Château de Brécy, Normandy, The Home of M. and Mme.
Jacques de Lacretelle." *Country Life*, June 17, 1976, pp. 1614-1617.

Allan BRAHAM and Peter SMITH. *François Mansart*.
London: A. Zwemmer, 1973.

Elizabetta CEREGHINI. *Brécy : Gentilhommière et Jardins*.
Aubervilliers, France: Boulingrin, 1996.

Philippe DETERVILLE. *Fermes, Manoirs et Châteaux du Bessin*.
Caen : Maître Jacques à Caen (Collection Normandie), 1999.

Kristie FERGUSSON. "The Long View." *The World of Interiors*,
n°. 43, June 1999, pp. 56-63.

J.C.N. FORESTIER. "Les Terrasses de Brécy." *La Vie à la campagne*,
vol. 2, n° 19, July 1, 1907.

Claude FREGNAC. *Merveilles des châteaux de Normandie*.
Paris: Hachette (Collection Réalités), 1966.

Dennis GUILLEMIN and Marie-Hélène SINCE. "Une histoire de l'art
des jardins." *Vieilles Maisons Françaises*, n° 77, April 1999.

A. HALLAYS. "En flânant entre Caen et Bayeux."
Le Journal des Débats, December 13, 1912.

Jacques de LACRETELLE. "La destinée d'un château historique –
Brécy en Calvados." *Vieilles Maisons Françaises*, n° 42.

Jacques de LACRETELLE. "Notre aventure à Brécy – Un aventure d'amour." *Connaissance des Arts*, n° 96, February 1960.

Jacques de LACRETELLE. "Cinq châteaux normands entre Bayeux et Caen." *Association de Basse-Normandie*, special number, 1st trimester, 1966.

Ed LAMBERT. *Notice historique sur la Ville, l'arrondissement et quelques communes limitrophes de Bayeux.* Paris: Imprimerie Renou et Maulde, 1862.

Jean de LA VARENDE. *Châteaux de Normandie, Itinéraire sentimental.* Paris: Plon, 1958.

Marie LE GAZIOU and Guillaume PELLERIN. *La Normandie des jardins.* Rennes: Éditions Ouest-France, 1999.

André MOLLET. *Le Jardin de Plaisir.* Paris : Editions du Moniteur, 1981. Facsimile edition of the original 1651 edition, printed in Stockholm.

Jacques MERLES. *Parcs et Jardins de Basse-Normandie.* Paris: Editions Duchamp-Chevalier, 1994.

Ian PHILLIPS. "Jardin de Brécy – Heavenward." *Veranda*, March-April, 2002, pp. 152-163.

Jacques POUGHEOL. "Parcs, promenades et jardins privés de Basse-Normandie." *Art de Basse-Normandie*, 1st trimester, 1996.

Philippe. SEYDOUX *La Normandie des châteaux et des manoirs.* Paris: Le Chêne, 1989.

H. SOLANGE-BODIN. "Les châteaux de Normandie", vol. 1, 1928.

Marie-Françoise VALÉRY. *Splendeurs des Jardins de Normandie.* Paris: Flammarion, 1995.

Marie-Françoise VALÉRY. "Normandie : Le Jardin de Brécy." *Maison et Jardin*, November 1995

Marie-Françoise VALÉRY. "Brécy ou le Poème en Vert." AD (French Edition of *Architectural Digest*), April 2000.

[Collection dirigée par Évelyne Demey]
Avec la collaboration de Sylviane Degunst

Direction artistique et maquette : Stéphanie Viau
Photogravure : GCS
Impression : Arta Grafica, Roumanie

© Eric T. Haskell for the text.

[Crédits photos]

Pascal Hinous, couverture (haut, bas), p.1, 3, 4 (gauche, milieu), 5, 9 (gauche), 12, 13, 14, 15, 16, 17, 19, 21, 22-23, 27, 28 (milieu, droite), 29, 30-31, 33, 40, 41, 43 (en haut à gauche, au milieu à droite, en bas à gauche), 45, 47, 48, 49, 50, 51, 53, 55, 56, 58, 61, 62, 64, 65, 66, 67, 71, 72, 75, 76, 77, 79, 80, 81, 82-83

Eric T. Haskell, p. 4 (droite), 5 (gauche), 8, 9 (droite), 20, 26, 28 (gauche), 34, 35, 36, 39, 43 (en bas : au milieu et à droite), 44, 46, 68-69, 73, 84

Cyril Nicolas, p. 10.

Dessin et lithographie par A. Maugendre, p. 24-25

[Acknowledgements]

No monograph has yet to appear on Brécy, and very little has been written on the château and gardens in English. For this reason, I am honored to have been encouraged by Didier and Barbara Wirth to compose this text. It was a great pleasure to collaborate with Evelyne Demey, director of Les Editions du Huitème Jour, whose enthusiasm and patience have made this project possible. I am also indebted to Dr. James J. Yoch for having read the manuscript with care. This monograph was written in honor of my Mother and Father.

This volume was first published in both French and English editions in 2007.

© Huitième Jour éditions, 2008
3 rue Séguier — 75006 Paris
ISBN : 9782914119757

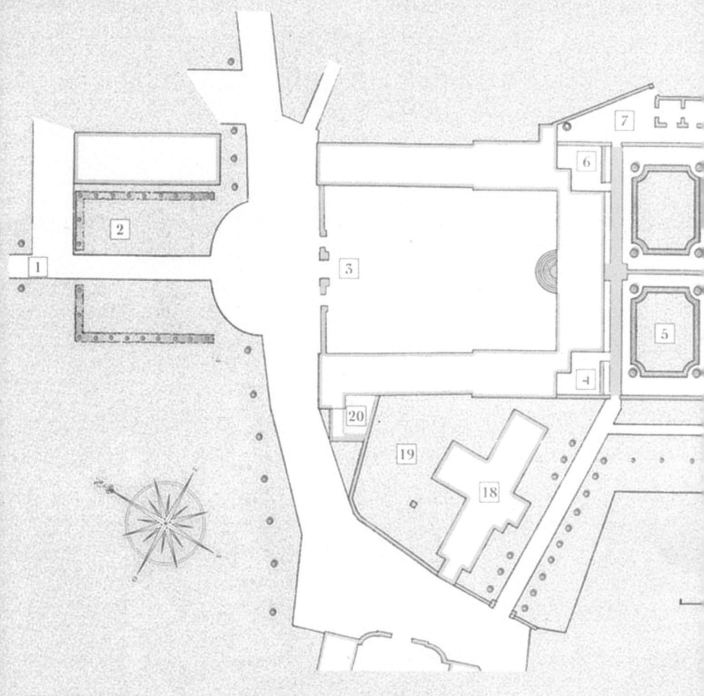